Peruvegan

Vicki Cosio

ISBN: 10: 1495385280
ISBN-13: 978-1495385285

DEDICATION

This book is dedicated to the billions of animals that needlessly suffer at the hands of humans every year....... in the hopes that someday, humans will make the connection and realize......that the most violent weapon on earth is their fork.

Introduction

I have wanted to write a vegan Peruvian cookbook for quite some time. But like most people, could not find the time because life was so busy. Every day was jam packed with work, taking care of a household, my husband, and my two (and at one point five) rescue dogs. Add in working out and training (I'm a nationally ranked tennis player), hiking with my dogs and cooking. It didn't leave much time for a cookbook, let alone sleep! I recently retired from my job, and decided my cookbook project was way overdue!

People arrive at veganism by many different paths. My husband and I became vegan, because of our great love for animals. We initially went vegetarian for a year and a half. After reading about the horrors inflicted by the dairy and egg industry, and the inhumane treatment of the animals, we went vegan overnight. That was fourteen years ago. It was the best decision we ever made in our lives.

So why vegan Peruvian food? Well, my husband is a native of Peru. Peru is well known for their meat centered diet, which is also heavy on the eggs and cheese. In many Peruvian dishes, eggs top the dishes as decoration. Not only is their traditional cuisine not the healthiest, but it's also not the kindest. I have been making vegan Peruvian food for my husband since we went vegan. You will never miss the meat, eggs or dairy in my recipes. My husband always tells me that my vegan versions are much more delicious than the traditional fare he grew up with. Who can go wrong when creamy Garlic Cashew Cheese is substituted for Queso Fresco?

I've renamed many of the traditional Peruvian dishes, to highlight their kinder, gentler, vegan versions (Lomito Saltado is now No Meat-o Saltado, Arroz Con Pollo is now Arroz Con Soy-o and Ocopa is now Fauxcopa.....just to name a few).

So if you can't afford to take a trip to Machu Picchu, go to the kitchen, put on some traditional Peruvian music and enjoy your culinary journey to the magical country of Peru!

CONTENTS

ACKNOWLEDGMENTS

I have to thank my most wonderful husband and two pups, for being the best tasters a cookbook author could ask for.

1. CRUCIAL CONDIMENTS

Once you try these condiments, you'll wonder how you ever survived in life without them. Creamy, delicious, savory and heavenly, try not to eat them by themselves! Although some of the condiments are technically not Peruvian, they take the place of many animal products that are used in the traditional recipes of Peru. They will pump up your dishes and take them to the next level!

CREAMY CILANTRO SAUCE

I created this luscious and creamy cilantro sauce, to serve on top of No Meat-o Saltado. However, this would taste wonderful on many of the dishes in this cookbook.

¾ cup of Vegan Garlic Aioli (see page 12)
½ bunch of fresh cilantro, lower stems removed
Unsweetened soy milk or almond milk

Place Vegan Garlic Aioli, cilantro and just enough soy milk (to make a medium sauce) into a blender and blend.

Makes approximately ¾ cup.

Creamy Cilantro Sauce on top of No Meat-o Saltado

GARLIC CASHEW CHEESE

Oh my!!! Wait until you try this. You will wake up thinking about what you are going to make, just so you can put cashew cheese on it!! It's delicious ON anything and delicious when ADDED to anything.

2 cups raw cashew pieces (soaked in water overnight)
½ cup water
1 ½ tablespoons rice vinegar (unseasoned) or apple cider vinegar
3 tablespoons nutritional yeast
1 ¼ tablespoons of mellow red miso
5 – 8 cloves of garlic
1 teaspoon of salt (or to taste)
Dash of agave nectar (optional)

Combine all ingredients in a blender or food processor.

You can also add a big handful of rehydrated sundried tomatoes, for Sundried Tomato Cashew Cheese. Or, you can add chopped fresh chives for Garlic Chive Cashew Cheese.

Makes approximately 1 ½ cups.

Garlic Cashew Cheese

GOLF

This super easy condiment is usually served with potatoes. It's also great spread on veggie burgers and sandwiches.

¾ cup Vegan Garlic Aioli (see page 12)
3 tablespoons vegan ketchup
Dash of aji amarillo paste (optional)

Combine all ingredients in a bowl and serve.

Makes approximately 1 cup.

Golf

ONION CRIOLLO SALSA

Like onions and spice? Try this on sandwiches, veggies, grains or potatoes.

1 yellow onion, sliced thinly into crescents
1 ½ cups vegetable broth (heated until almost boiling)
½ tablespoon aji panca paste
½ tablespoon aji amarillo paste
Juice of one lime
1/3 cup chopped cilantro

Combine all ingredients except cilantro. Allow to marinate for approximately 30 minutes. Add cilantro and serve.

Makes approximately 1 ½ cups.

Onion Criollo Salsa atop Papa Rellena

SALSA VERDE

This aji sauce can be made to your taste. You can make it as hot or as mild as you like. Feel free to play around with the measurements of all of the ingredients. Serve it with stews, soups, grains, or pasta, or as a dip for bread.

¼ cup olive oil
Juice of 2 limes
1 large bunch of cilantro
1 teaspoon salt
2 teaspoons aji amarillo paste
1 tablespoon Vegan Garlic Aioli (see page 12)

Blend all ingredients in a blender.

Makes approximately 1 cup.

Salsa Verde

VEGAN GARLIC AIOLI

This is a creamy condiment that once you have it, you can't stop thinking about it. Especially delicious on stews, soups, and rice dishes, but equally delicious on sandwiches. You might want to double the recipe!

¼ cup soy milk
3 cloves of garlic, minced
2/3 cup canola oil
¾ teaspoon apple cider vinegar
½ to 1 teaspoon of salt (to taste)

Place soy milk and garlic in a blender. Use the lowest speed possible. If you have a "stir" setting, that works great. Blend soy milk and garlic. With the blender running, add the canola oil one tablespoon at a time, pouring it in as slowly as possible. Keep the blender running, until you have incorporated all of the oil and the mixture is the consistency of mayonnaise. Add cider vinegar and salt and blend. Spoon on top of just about everything and enjoy!

Makes approximately ¾ cup.

Vegan Garlic Aioli

VEGAN PARMESAN

With just the right amount of saltiness and sharpness, this parmesan will take your dishes to the next level.

1 cup of walnut "powder" (whole raw walnuts pulverized in a blender or food processor)
2/3 cup of nutritional yeast
1 ½ teaspoons of salt (or to taste)

Put all ingredients into a glass jar with a lid and shake.

Makes approximately 1 2/3 cup.

Vegan Parmesan

2. APPETIZERS & SIDES

Guenazo!!! Peruvian slang for "super good" and that's what you'll think about these appetizers and sides!!!

BAKED YUCCA FRIES

Yucca, also known as cassava, is a starchy root vegetable. Similar to a potato but slightly sweeter and sturdier, it makes fantastic fries.

2 large yucca (approximately 2.5 lbs)
1 ½ tablespoons olive oil
½ teaspoon smoked paprika
½ teaspoon salt
Golf (see page 6)

Preheat oven to 400 degrees. Line a cookie sheet with parchment paper.

Peel yucca. Cut into 3" pieces. Place pieces in large pot. Cover with water. Bring to boil over high heat. Reduce heat to low and cover. Allow to cook for approximately ten minutes. Remove from heat and drain. Allow to cool to room temperature.

Remove tough inner fiber from the middle of the yucca pieces. Slice into fries. Place on parchment lined cookie sheet. Sprinkle with smoked paprika and salt. Add olive oil and toss to coat. Bake until golden, approximately ten minutes. Turn fries over and bake until golden on the other side, approximately ten minutes. Season to taste with salt and paper. Serve fries with Golf.

Serves 4

Baked Yucca Fries

CREMA DE ZAPALLO

Try this cream of butternut squash soup, when winter squashes are at their peak. This soup is a cinch to make. Comfy and cozy on a winter's night. Great as a first course for company. Pumped up with cilantro and Garlic Cashew Cheese.

2 cups peeled and diced butternut squash (raw)
2 ½ cups of vegetable broth
½ cup soy milk
½ teaspoon cumin
¾ teaspoon salt
1 tablespoon Garlic Cashew Cheese (see page 4)
½ cup cilantro

Place butternut squash and broth in a large pot. Bring to boil over high heat. Reduce heat to medium low and simmer until tender, approximately 15 to 20 minutes. Add soy milk, cumin, salt and Garlic Cashew Cheese. Allow to cool. When mixture is no longer hot, place all ingredients into a blender. Add cilantro and blend. Season to taste with salt and pepper.

Serves 4

Crema de Zapallo

ENSALADA DE PALLARES

Lima bean, tomato and onion salad, topped with cilantro and a creamy dressing. Can be served cold or at room temperature.

1 16 oz. package of frozen lima beans
1 onion, diced
1 tablespoon olive oil
3 tomatoes, coarsely chopped
1 tablespoon aji amarillo paste
1 teaspoon oregano
1 ½ teaspoons salt
Cilantro for garnish, chopped

DRESSING

½ cup reserved lima beans
½ cup Vegan Garlic Aioli (see page 12)
½ cup cilantro, chopped
½ cup soy milk
½ teaspoon salt

Place frozen lima beans in a soup pot and add ½ cup of water. Bring to a boil. Reduce heat and cook until tender, approximately 15 minutes. Remove from heat and set aside. Allow to cool to room temperature.

In large fry pan over medium heat, cook onion in olive oil until translucent. Add tomatoes, aji amarillo paste, oregano and salt. Cook for an additional two minutes. Remove from heat. Add all but ½ cup of the lima beans to the tomato mixture and stir. Season to taste with salt and pepper.

Place all dressing ingredients in a blender and combine.

Plate the bean, tomato and onion mixture. Drizzle the dressing over the top. Garnish with extra chopped cilantro.

Serves 4

Ensalada de Pallares

PALTA RELLENA

Hollowed out avocado halves, filled with a creamy mixture of cooked vegetables and Vegan Garlic Aioli. Perfect for company because the dish is so pretty!

2 avocados
1 lime
2 cups of cooked vegetables (I like to use cooked carrots, corn, peas, and raw tomato)
½ cup of Vegan Garlic Aioli (see page 12)
Salt and pepper
1 cup of sunflower sprouts

Cut the avocados in half and peel away the skin. Remove the pit. Take a spoon and hollow out a little more of the avocado halves, to make the center a little bigger. Sprinkle with a little of the lime juice and sprinkle with salt and pepper.

In a bowl, mixed the cooked vegetables and raw tomato with the Vegan Garlic Aioli. Add salt and pepper to taste.

Place vegetable mixture inside of the hollowed out avocado halves. Top with sunflower
sprouts.

Serves 4

Palta Rellena

PAPAS A LA HUANCAINA

Traditionally the potatoes in this dish are boiled. I like to roast the potatoes, then pour the sauce over them. The roasting brings out the sweetness in the potatoes.

5 medium to large yellow skinned potatoes, cut into wedges
1 tablespoon olive oil
½ teaspoon of sea salt
1 tablespoon olive oil
1 onion, diced
1 ¾ teaspoons turmeric
1 garlic clove, minced
1 ½ tablespoons Sriracha sauce or other red hot pepper sauce
2 cups raw cashews, soaked overnight
1 tablespoon mellow red miso
5 tablespoons nutritional yeast
1 cup of unsweetened almond milk or soy milk
1 ½ cups of water
1 tablespoon of sea salt

Preheat oven to 400 degrees. Mix cut potatoes with olive oil and season with salt and pepper. Place on parchment lined baking sheet and roast for approximately 30 to 40 minutes, or until browned on the outside.

In the meantime, prepare the sauce. In a large frying pan, sauté onion in olive oil over medium heat until translucent. Add turmeric, garlic and Sriracha sauce. Sauté for another five minutes. Remove from heat.

In a blender combine the onion mixture, cashews, miso, nutritional yeast, almond milk, water and sea salt. Blend thoroughly.

Pour sauce over cooked potatoes and garnish with sliced olives. Season to taste with salt and pepper.

Serves 6 to 8

Papas a la Huancaina

ROASTED PERUVIAN PURPLE POTATOES

These potatoes are so colorful, they are a great addition to any dish or just to eat as an appetizer. Roasted in olive oil with rosemary……….yum! If eating as an appetizer, they are great served alongside Golf and Salsa Verde.

1 ½ pounds Peruvian purple potatoes, cut into cubes
1 tablespoon olive oil
1 tablespoon minced fresh rosemary
¾ teaspoon salt
½ teaspoon pepper
Golf (see page 6)
Salsa Verde (see page 10)

Preheat oven to 375 degrees. Line baking sheet with parchment paper.

Place potatoes on baking sheet. Toss with olive oil, rosemary, salt and pepper. Roast until golden brown, approximately 35 minutes. Season to taste with salt and pepper.

Serve with Golf and Salsa Verde.

Serves 4

Roasted Peruvian Purple Potatoes

VICKI COSIO

3. MAIN DISHES

Que rico! Peruvian speak for "super delicious." These main dishes will have you learning Spanish in no time...........well, at least you will be shouting "que rico" a lot. Easy enough for every day meals, but fancy enough for company.

AJI DE SOYLLINA (AJI DE GALLINA)

This is my Peruvian husband's favorite dish, hands down. It was his favorite as a kid, and still is as an adult. This spicy, creamy and cheesy stew, is made up of ground walnuts, soy milk and bread paste. It's traditionally made with chicken. If you don't want to add fake chicken strips, you can substitute roasted potatoes and add them once the sauce is done.

5 slices of vegan white bread, crusts removed

2 cups of soy milk

¼ cup of olive oil

1 onion, diced

2 cloves of garlic, minced

1 ½ cups of vegan fake chicken strips

¼ cup aji amarillo paste

1 tablespoon aji panca paste

2 teaspoons salt

1 cup walnuts, ground in a blender or food processor

1 cup of vegetable broth

1 cup of soy milk

½ cup nutritional yeast

2 tablespoons Garlic Cashew Cheese (see page 4)

1 tablespoon evaporated cane juice

In a large bowl, tear the bread into pieces and add soy milk. Mash down with a fork. Allow to sit for approximately 15 minutes. Mash again so that the bread breaks down. Set aside.

In a large skillet over medium heat, sauté onions, garlic and fake chicken strips in olive oil. Sauté until the onions are translucent and the strips are brown. Add aji amarillo paste, aji panca paste, salt and walnuts. Sauté for another two to three minutes. Add vegetable broth, soy milk, nutritional yeast and reserved bread and soy milk mixture. Bring to a simmer. Allow to simmer over low heat for approximately ten minutes. Add Garlic Cashew Cheese and evaporated cane juice. Simmer for another few minutes, until the cheese and evaporated cane juice has been incorporated. Season to taste with salt and pepper. Serve over rice.

Serves 4

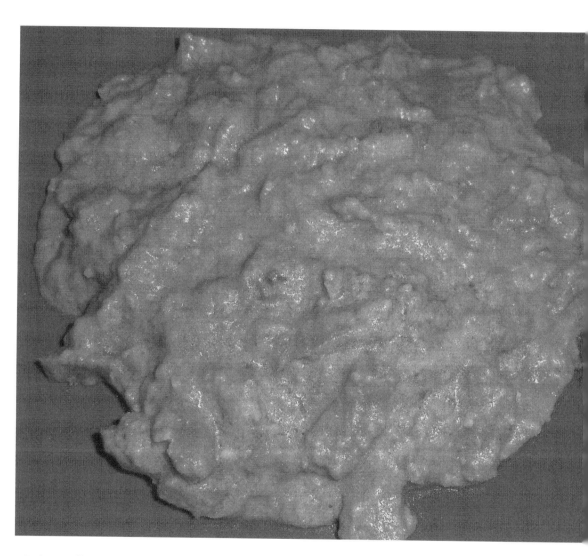

Aji de Soyllina (Aji de Gallina)

AJIACO DE PAPAS

A delicious and creamy potato dish. Potatoes originated in Peru, which is why they have so many potato dishes! Garlic Cashew Cheese and soy or nut milk replaces the cream and cheese in the original version. This dish is served next to a side of rice. This dish can also be served as an appetizer or side dish.

2 tablespoons olive oil
1 onion, diced
2 tablespoons aji amarillo paste
½ teaspoon smoked paprika
½ teaspoon turmeric
1 cup water
2 teaspoons Bragg's Liquid Aminos
4 medium yellow or white potatoes, peeled and diced
¾ cup soy milk or nut milk
½ cup Garlic Cashew Cheese (see page 4)
1 teaspoon salt

In large fry pan over medium heat, sauté onion in olive oil until translucent. Add aji amarillo paste, smoked paprika and turmeric. Stir fry for another minute. Add water, Bragg's Liquid Aminos and potatoes. Bring to a boil. Reduce heat, cover and simmer until tender, approximately 20-25 minutes. Add soy milk, Garlic Cashew Cheese and salt. Remove from heat. Season to taste with additional salt and pepper.

Serves 4

Ajiaco de Papas

A-NO-NO CHANCHO (ADOBO CHANCHO)

Peruvian adobos are like nothing you've ever tried before. The longer this simmers to absorb the flavors, the better it gets! You can substitute some of the beer with vegetable broth if desired. Serve over rice with steamed greens.

2 onions, sliced into thin rounds
1 ½ cups seitan, cubed
2 tablespoons olive oil
2 cloves of garlic, minced
1 ½ teaspoons cumin
1 teaspoon smoked paprika
2 bay leaves
2 whole allspice
3 cups of light colored beer or ale
½ cup aji panca paste
1 tablespoon of cider vinegar
1 cup of fresh or frozen (and thawed) corn kernels, blended with 1 cup of vegetable broth
2 teaspoons of evaporated cane juice
1 tablespoon of vegetable bouillon base
Vegan Garlic Aioli (see page 12)

In large fry pan over medium heat, sauté onions and seitan in olive oil. Cook, stirring frequently, until the onions turn translucent. Add garlic, cumin, smoked paprika, bay leaves and allspice and stir for two more minutes. Add beer, aji panca paste, vinegar, corn/broth mixture and evaporated cane juice. Bring to a boil over medium high heat. Reduce heat to low, cover and simmer for one hour. Add the vegetable bouillon base and simmer for an additional 40 minutes. Season to taste with salt and pepper. Serve over rice with a dollop of Vegan Garlic Aioli.

Serves 4

A-No-No Chancho (Adobo Chancho)

ARROZ A LA JARDINERA

This dish translates to "garden rice." It's best made with Indian basmati white rice, to showcase the color of the dish. You can pump it up with the addition of seitan. Or, crumble and brown some tempeh, and add it to the finished rice. Since this dish traditionally includes cooked egg, you can also brown some tofu in olive oil, crumble it by hand, and add it to the rice prior to fluffing it with a fork.

2 tablespoons olive oil
1 onion, diced
1 clove of garlic, minced
1 cup fresh or frozen corn kernels
1 cup fresh or frozen peas
1 carrot, diced
2 teaspoon cumin
½ teaspoon smoked paprika
2 teaspoons turmeric
2 teaspoons salt
2 ½ tablespoons aji amarillo paste
2 cups Indian basmati rice (white)

In large fry pan over medium heat, sauté onions and garlic in olive oil. Cook, stirring frequently, until the onions turn translucent. Add corn, peas and carrot. Sauté for two more minutes. Add cumin, smoked paprika, turmeric, salt and aji amarillo paste. Sauté for another minute. Add 3 ¼ cups of water to the pan and bring to a boil. Add rice. Bring to a boil again. Reduce heat to medium low, cover and cook until rice is tender (approximately 15 minutes). Remove from heat and allow to rest for 10 minutes. Fluff with a fork. Season to taste with salt and pepper and serve.

Serves 4

Arroz a la Jardinera

ARROZ CON SOY-O (ARROZ CON POLLO)

A very traditional and popular dish of Peru. In this version, soy chicken strips, rice and spices are cooked in beer. When the rice has absorbed all of the liquid, a cilantro sauce is added for extra flavor and color. If you prefer a lighter tasting dish, vegetable broth may be substituted for half of the beer.

2 ½ cups of vegan fake chicken strips
2 tablespoons olive oil
2 teaspoons cumin
1 tablespoon fresh lemon juice
3 ½ cups of pale ale or beer
1 teaspoon of sea salt
2 cups of white Indian basmati rice
1 large bunch of cilantro (bottom stems removed)
½ cup of water

In large skillet over medium heat, cook fake chicken strips in olive oil until browned on both sides. Add 2 teaspoons of cumin and stir for another minute. Add lemon juice, the ale/beer, salt and rice. Bring to a boil over high heat, cover, and reduce heat to low. Simmer until the rice has absorbed all of the liquid, approximately 20-25 minutes. In the meantime, blend cilantro and water in a blender until it's the consistency of a sauce. Set aside. When the rice has absorbed all of the liquid, remove from heat and let rest (covered) for 5-10 minutes. Add cilantro sauce and mix well. Season to taste with salt and pepper.

Note: You can also add 1 cup of fresh or frozen peas to the dish while it's cooking.

Serves 4

Arroz con Soy-o (Arroz con Pollo)

BLACK BEAN WALNUT BURGERS WITH PERUVIAN SPICES

These burgers are fantastic in both flavor and texture. Serve them on a bun with your favorite condiments, or inside of lettuce leaves topped with Garlic Cashew Cheese.

1 ½ cups cooked black beans
4 tablespoons Bragg's Liquid Aminos
2/3 cup chopped walnuts
2 tablespoons nutritional yeast
2 ½ tablespoons ground flaxseeds
Several drops of liquid smoke
1/3 cup chopped onion
1/3 cup chopped red pepper
1/3 cup chopped carrots
2 teaspoons cumin
1 teaspoon smoked paprika
1 teaspoon garlic powder
1/2 cup chopped fresh cilantro
2/3 cup vital wheat gluten flour
Olive oil for cooking

Mash black beans well with a fork, until it resembles refried beans. Add other ingredients. Shape into 4 large burgers or 8 small burgers. Pan fry/sauté in olive oil (or coconut oil) until nicely browned on both sides. Season to taste with salt and pepper.

Serves 4

Black Bean Walnut Burgers with Peruvian Spices

CARAPULCRA

A lovely stew with exotic spices, made even more luscious with the addition of peanut butter. Serve over rice or quinoa with steamed greens.

1 ½ cups of seitan, cubed
1 onion, diced
2 cloves of garlic, minced
2 tablespoons olive oil
1 teaspoon cumin
½ teaspoon cinnamon
½ teaspoon garam masala
2 teaspoons aji panca paste
1 teaspoon aji amarillo paste
½ teaspoon salt
3 cups water
¼ cup dry red wine
1 tablespoon of vegetable bouillon base
5 small red potatoes, diced
3 tablespoons crunchy peanut butter
½ cup chopped fresh cilantro
Evaporated cane juice (to taste)

In a large fry pan over medium heat, cook the seitan, onion and garlic in olive oil until the onions turn translucent. Add cumin, cinnamon, garam masala, aji panca paste, aji amarillo paste and salt. Stir for another two minutes. Add water, wine, bouillon base and potatoes. Bring to a boil, cover and reduce heat to low. Simmer until potatoes are cooked through, approximately 20-25 minutes. Remove approximately ½ cup of hot broth from the stew, and place it into a mug. Add the peanut butter and stir until it's incorporated into the broth. Return the mixture to the stew and stir thoroughly. Remove from heat. Add chopped fresh cilantro. Season to taste with salt, pepper and a little evaporated cane juice.

Serves 4

Carapulcra

ESTOFADO

A super tasty stew simmered in a vegetable broth and wine sauce, additionally flavored with bay leaves, aji amarillo paste and tomato paste. Don't forget to pour yourself some wine while you are cooking the stew. The stew can't have all the fun!

1 onion, diced
1 clove of garlic, minced
2 tablespoons olive oil
1 ½ cups seitan, cubed
3 bay leaves
1 ½ tablespoons aji amarillo paste
2 cups of vegetable broth
½ cup dry red wine
½ cup port wine
1 ½ tablespoons tomato paste
1 teaspoon salt
½ teaspoon pepper
1 tablespoon evaporated cane juice
3 medium potatoes, diced
Vegan Garlic Aioli (see page 12)

In large fry pan over medium heat, sauté onion, garlic, and seitan in olive oil until the onion turns translucent. Add the bay leaves and aji amarillo paste and sauté for another minute. Add broth, red wine, port wine, tomato paste, salt, pepper, evaporated cane juice and potatoes. Bring to a boil. Reduce heat and cover. Simmer until the potatoes are done, approximately 30 minutes. Season to taste with salt and pepper. Serve over rice. Top with Vegan Garlic Aioli.

Serves 3-4

Estofado

FAUXCOPA (OCOPA)

Peruvians love their potatoes, and you will love this dish! Roasted potatoes topped with a creamy, cheesy, peanut sauce. This dish can be served as a main course with a side vegetable or salad, or as an appetizer.

4 large yellow skinned potatoes, cubed
½ tablespoon olive oil
1 onion, diced
2 cloves of garlic, minced
2 tablespoons aji amarillo paste
¼ cup of minced fresh cilantro and minced fresh mint (equal amounts to equal ¼ cup)
½ cup of peanut butter
1 ¼ cups soy milk
½ cup Garlic Cashew Cheese (see page 4)
3 vegan vanilla sandwich cookies (filling removed)
1 ½ teaspoons salt

Preheat oven to 400 degrees. On a parchment lined baking sheet, place the cubed potatoes. Rub with olive oil. Roast until golden brown, approximately 35-40 minutes. Set aside.

In a large fry pan over medium heat, saute the onion and garlic in olive oil until the onion turns translucent. Add the aji amarillo paste and the fresh herbs. Sauté for 30 seconds and remove from heat. Set aside.

In a blender place the peanut butter, soy milk, Garlic Cashew Cheese, cookies, salt and reserved vegetables. Blend. Season to taste with salt and pepper. Pour sauce over cooked potatoes.

Serves 4

Fauxcopa (Ocopa)

FAUXNDONGUITO A LA ITALIANA (MONDONGUITO A LA ITALIANA)

A seitan stir fry with an Italian influence. Topped with Vegan Parmesan Cheese, it is traditionally served over rice. I won't tell if you want to serve it over pasta, as it's equally delicious that way!

5-6 medium yellow skinned potatoes, cut into fries
1 tablespoon olive oil
½ teaspoon cumin
½ teaspoon salt
2 tablespoons olive oil
1 onion, diced
1 ½ cups of seitan (sliced into strips)
3 cloves of garlic, minced
2 bay leaves
½ tablespoon of evaporated cane juice
½ tablespoon aji amarillo paste
2 tablespoons tomato paste
1 ½ cups veggie broth or 1 ½ cups of water plus 2 teaspoons of vegetable bouillon base
½ cup of fresh or frozen peas
Vegan Parmesan (see page 14)

Preheat oven to 400 degrees. Slice the potatoes into fries. Place on a parchment lined baking sheet. Add olive oil, salt, cumin and mix. Bake at 400 degrees for approximately 20 minutes or until golden brown. Remove from oven and set aside.

In a large fry pan over medium heat, cook the onion and seitan in olive oil until translucent. Add garlic, bay leaves, evaporated cane juice, aji amarillo paste, tomato paste, broth and peas. Bring to a boil. Reduce heat to low and simmer for 5 to 10 minutes to blend the flavors. Add the French fries and stir. Season to taste with salt and pepper. Sprinkle with Vegan Parmesan.

Serves 4

Fauxndonguito a la Italiana (Mondonguito a la Italiana)

GREEN & NOT MEAN SPAGHETTI (TALLARIN VERDE)

This pesto sauce is so much lighter and better tasting than traditional pesto. And without any added oil and the addition of spinach, it's much healthier than the traditional version. Just try not to lick the blender when you are done.

1 onion, diced
1 tablespoon olive oil
2 cloves of garlic, minced
1 tablespoon of aji amarillo paste
½ cup of soy milk or nut milk
3 cups of packed fresh spinach
1 cup of packed fresh basil
¼ cup of walnuts
¼ cup of nutritional yeast
2 teaspoons salt
¼ cup Garlic Cashew Cheese (see page 4)
1 pound of cooked spaghetti

In large fry pan over medium heat, sauté onion in olive oil until translucent. Add garlic and aji amarillo paste, and saute for another two minutes. Remove from heat and add contents to a blender or food processor. Add soy milk, spinach, basil, walnuts, nutritional yeast, salt, and Garlic Cashew Cheese. Blend. Season to taste with salt and pepper. Serve over cooked spaghetti.

Serves 4

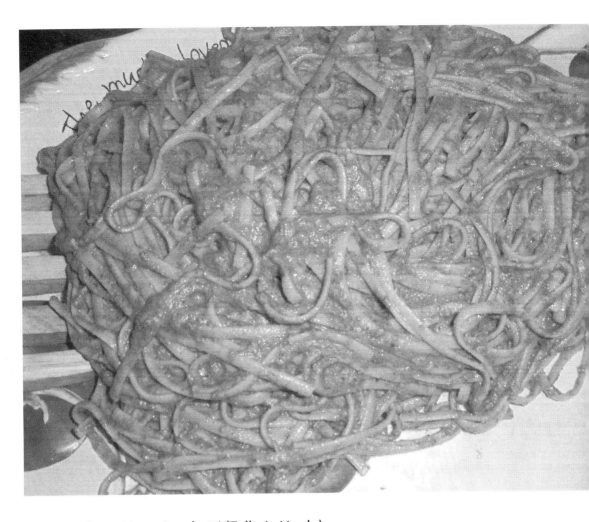

Green and Not Mean Spaghetti (Tallarin Verde)

GUMBO PERUVIAN STYLE

This is how I think gumbo would taste, if it was a traditional dish of Peru. With vegan chorizo, vegetables, cumin and cilantro. A great dish for company, since you can make it ahead of time and it tastes even more delicious the next day.

3 tablespoons olive oil
1/3 cup olive oil
1/3 cup flour
4 cups vegetable broth
1 red bell pepper, chopped
3 stalks of celery, chopped
1 16 oz. package of frozen sweet white corn
1 medium zucchini, chopped
1 16oz. can of chopped tomatoes
3 garlic cloves, minced
2 bay leaves
½ teaspoon cumin
1 teaspoon basil
1 ½ teaspoons salt
1 ¼ teaspoons of gumbo file powder
Splash of liquid smoke
½ cup fresh cilantro, chopped
Vegan Garlic Aioli (see page 12)

In large skillet over medium heat, cook vegan chorizo in three tablespoons of olive until browned and crispy. Remove from pan and set aside. To the same pan over medium low heat, add 1/3 cup of olive oil and 1/3 cup of flour. Stir constantly until browned. Add vegetable broth, bell pepper, celery, corn, zucchini, tomatoes, garlic, bay leaves, cumin, basil, salt and liquid smoke. Add ½ of the cooked vegan chorizo. Bring mixture to a low boil, reduce heat, cover half way and simmer for approximately 15-20 minutes. Add gumbo file and the remaining vegan chorizo. Simmer for another 10 minutes. Remove from heat, and add ½ cup of chopped cilantro. Season to taste with salt and pepper. Serve over rice with Vegan Garlic Aioli or vegan sour cream.

Serves 6

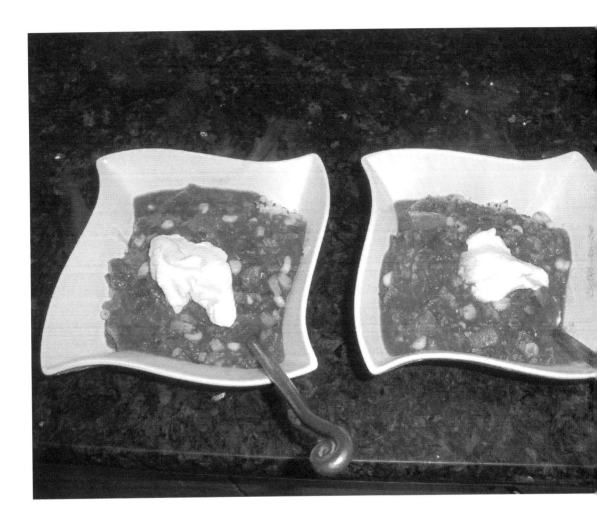

Gumbo Peruvian Style

LOCRO

This stew is the ultimate in "yum" and the best way to enjoy winter squash. The finished dish is like eating a bowl of creamy mashed potatoes and butternut squash.

2 cups peeled and diced butternut squash (raw)
2 cups vegan no-chicken broth or vegetable broth
1 onion, diced
2 tablespoons olive oil
2 cloves of garlic, minced
2 tablespoons aji amarillo paste
1 tablespoon aji panca paste
1 teaspoon cumin
1 ½ teaspoons salt
1 cup soy milk or nut milk
3 medium yellow skinned potatoes, diced
1 cup fresh or frozen corn
½ cup fresh or frozen peas
Soy milk, as needed
½ cup Garlic Cashew Cheese (see page 4)

Place butternut squash and broth in a medium pot. Bring to boil over high heat. Reduce heat to medium low, cover and simmer until tender, approximately 15 minutes. Remove from heat and allow to cool. Place contents in a blender and blend. Set aside.

In a large soup pot over medium heat, cook onion in olive oil until translucent. Add garlic, aji amarillo paste, aji panca paste, cumin and salt. Cook for two minutes. Add butternut squash puree, soy milk, potatoes, corn and peas. Bring to a boil. Reduce heat to low, cover and simmer until the potatoes are tender, approximately 20-25 minutes. Remove from heat. Add additional soy milk, if a thinner stew is desired. Add Garlic Cashew Cheese and stir until melted. Season to taste with salt and pepper. Serve over rice.

Serves 4 to 6

Locro

NO COW COW (CAU CAU)

Seitan replaces tripe in this dish, which is why it is called No Cow Cow. This delicious stew seasoned with typical Peruvian spices is served over rice. It would also be terrific served over a bed of red quinoa.

1 ½ cups seitan, sliced into strips
1 tablespoon olive oil
1 onion, sliced into crescents
2 tablespoons olive oil
2 cloves of garlic, minced
2 ½ tablespoons aji amarillo paste
2 teaspoons cumin
1 teaspoons turmeric
1 teaspoon sea salt
4 cups of vegan no chicken broth (you can also substitute a light colored vegetable broth)
3 medium yellow skinned potatoes, diced
1/3 cup fresh mint

In a large skillet over medium heat, cook the seitan in olive oil until browned on both sides. Remove from pan and set aside. Add onion and olive oil to the same pan and cook until the onion is translucent. Add garlic, aji amarillo paste, cumin, turmeric and sea salt. Sauté for a minute or two. Add broth and potatoes. Bring to a boil. Reduce heat to medium low. Cover and simmer until potatoes are tender, approximately 15 to 20 minutes. Remove from heat. Add seitan strips and mint. Season to taste with salt and pepper. Serve over rice or quinoa.

Serves 4

No Cow Cow (Cau Cau)

NO MEAT-O SALTADO (LOMITO SALTADO) WITH CREAMY CILANTRO SAUCE

You just can't go wrong with this dish. It never fails to impress when you make it for friends or family. Even the most picky eaters will slurp it up, faster than you can say "Peruvian.". A wonderful stir fry of seitan, tomatoes, onions, spices............and French fries. Yup, French fries!!!

1 ½ cups seitan strips
½ teaspoon smoked paprika
2 teaspoons cumin
½ teaspoon red pepper flakes
3 cloves garlic, minced
1 tablespoon olive oil
1 tablespoon balsamic vinegar
½ cup cilantro, minced
Dash of salt and pepper
5-6 medium yellow skinned potatoes, cut into fries
1 tablespoon olive oil
½ teaspoon smoked paprika
½ teaspoon garlic powder
1 tablespoon olive oil
1 onion, sliced into crescents
2 tablespoons balsamic vinegar
1 ½ tablespoons of vegetable bouillon base
3 cups water
2 tomatoes, chopped
Creamy Cilantro Sauce (see page 2)

Preheat oven to 400 degrees.

Combine seitan, paprika, cumin, red pepper flakes, garlic, olive oil, balsamic vinegar, cilantro, salt and pepper in a glass bowl. Allow to marinate at least one hour.

While the seitan is marinating, make the French fries. Slice potatoes into fries.

Place on a parchment lined baking sheet. Add olive oil, paprika and garlic powder and mix. Bake for approximately 20 minutes or until golden brown. Remove from oven and set aside.

In a large fry pan over medium heat, cook the marinated seitan and onion in the olive oil. Cook until the onions turn translucent. Add vinegar and stir fry for an additional minute. Add bouillon base, water and tomatoes. Bring to a boil. Reduce heat to low and simmer for approximately 5 minutes, until the base has dissolved. Add fries and mix thoroughly until heated through. Remove from heat. Season to taste with salt and pepper. Serve saltado over rice, topped with Creamy Cilantro Sauce.

Serves 4

No Meat-o Saltado (Lomito Saltado) with Creamy Cilantro Sauce

PAPA RELLENA

A seitan filling encircled by mashed potatoes, and formed into the shape of a whole potato. The "potato" is then rolled in bread crumbs and fried...........mmmmmmm.

7 medium unpeeled gold or brown skinned potatoes, cut into thirds
2 tablespoons garbanzo bean flour
1 tablespoon salt
2 tablespoons olive oil
1 onion, chopped
2 cloves of garlic, minced
1 ½ cups ground seitan
1 ½ teaspoons cumin
¾ teaspoon smoked paprika
1 tablespoon aji amarillo paste
1 tablespoon aji panca paste
1/3 cup chopped cilantro
¾ cup panko bread crumbs
Olive oil for cooking
Onion Criollo Sauce (see page 8)

Place potatoes in a large stock pot. Fill with water to cover. Bring to a boil over medium high heat. Reduce heat to medium low and simmer until cooked through, approximately 25 minutes. Mash potatoes with a potato masher. Add garbanzo bean flour and salt. Set aside and let cool.

While the potatoes are cooking, prepare the seitan and onion mixture. In a large fry pan over medium heat, sauté the onion in olive oil for approximately five minutes. Add garlic, seitan, cumin, paprika, aji amarillo paste and aji panca paste. Lower heat to medium low and cook for approximately 10 minutes, stirring frequently. Add a little vegetable broth or water, if the seitan mixture becomes too dry. Add cilantro and remove from heat. Set aside.

Scoop ¾ cup of mashed potatoes from the pot and form into a disk. Make a hollow in the center and fill with some of the seitan filling. Leave enough room so that you can enclose the potatoes around the filling. Shape into the size of a medium baked potato. Roll in panko bread crumbs. Repeat with the rest of the potatoes, until the filling or potatoes run out.

Pour olive oil in large fry pan, until it measures approximately one inch. Preheat olive oil for a few minutes. Fry potatoes over medium heat until browned and crispy on both sides. Use extra caution when you turn the potatoes over, as they are delicate. Season to taste with salt and pepper.

Serve hot with Onion Criollo Sauce and your favorite vegan gravy. Garnish with any leftover seitan filling.

Papa Rellena with Onion Criollo Sauce

PEPIAN DE CHOCLO WITH ROASTED BUTTERNUT SQUASH

This delicious stew has pureed corn as its base. I like to add roasted butternut squash for both color and texture. Even though the corn that's traditionally used in Peru is gigantic, regular corn works just as well.

3 cups of frozen sweet white corn
½ bunch of fresh cilantro
3 ½ cups vegetable broth
1 large onion, diced
2 tablespoons olive oil
1 clove of garlic, minced
1 teaspoon cumin
1 teaspoon turmeric
1 ½ teaspoons salt
1 ½ tablespoons aji amarillo paste
1 ½ cups of roasted butternut squash, cubed

Combine corn, cilantro and broth in a blender. Set aside.

In a large skillet over medium heat, cook onion in olive oil until translucent. Add garlic, cumin, turmeric, salt and aji amarillo paste. Cook for an additional minute or two. Add corn mixture to skillet. Cook over low heat for approximately 30 minutes. Add squash and heat through. Season to taste with salt and pepper. Serve with rice and additional aji amarillo paste.

Serves 4

Pepian de Choclo with Roasted Butternut Squash

PERUVIAN INSPIRED ROYRIZO SAUCE

My husband loves this pasta sauce so much made with vegan chorizo, that I named it "Royrizo Sauce" (since his name is Roy). Although not a traditional dish of Peru, it incorporates the flavors of the country. Even though the sauce is made for pasta, it would also be incredible over roasted potatoes.

1 12oz. package of vegan chorizo
2 tablespoons olive oil
1 tablespoon olive oil
1 red pepper, chopped
1 onion, chopped
1 ½ cups frozen sweet white corn
4 cups unsweetened soy milk or almond milk
½ cup walnuts (pulverized in a blender or food processor)
½ cup nutritional yeast
1 tablespoon vegetable bouillon base
1 teaspoon of salt
½ teaspoon of pepper
½ teaspoon red pepper flakes
1 cup of fresh spinach, chopped
1 tomato, chopped
¾ cup cilantro, chopped
1 pound of cooked pasta

In a large skillet over medium heat, pan fry vegan chorizo in 2 tablespoons of olive oil until crispy on the outside. Remove from pan. Add another tablespoon of olive oil to the pan. Sauté red pepper, onion and corn, until corn is heated through and vegetables are softened. Return vegan chorizo to the pan. Add soy milk or almond milk, walnuts, nutritional yeast, bouillon base, salt, pepper and red pepper flakes. Allow sauce to simmer over low heat for about ten minutes. Add chopped spinach and tomato and simmer for five more minutes. (You can add more or less soy milk/almond milk if you want a thicker or thinner sauce). Remove from heat, add cilantro and stir. Season to taste with salt and pepper. Serve over pasta.

Serves 4

Peruvian Inspired Royrizo Sauce

PERUVIAN PINTO PUREE

Wow. This dish comes together in about ten minutes, but tastes like you slaved all day over the stove. Nothing says comfort food better than bean puree. This puree tastes great over rice or quinoa.

1 onion, diced
1 tablespoon olive oil
Dash of agave nectar
1 15 oz. can of pinto beans (rinsed and drained)
1 ½ cups of vegetable broth
1 medium tomato
2 tablespoons nutritional yeast
1 teaspoon cumin
½ teaspoon smoked paprika
1 tablespoon aji panca paste
Couple dashes of liquid smoke
1 tablespoon olive oil
½ bunch cilantro, stems removed
Vegan Garlic Aioli (see page 12)

In a large fry pan over medium heat, sauté the onion in olive oil for approximately five minutes. Lower heat and keep cooking until lightly browned. Add a dash of agave nectar. Add the beans, broth, tomato, nutritional yeast, cumin, smoked paprika, aji panca paste and liquid smoke. Heat until warmed through. Allow to cool slightly. Place ingredients in a blender. Add olive oil and cilantro and blend. Season to taste with salt and pepper. Serve over rice with vegan sour cream or Vegan Garlic Aioli.

Serves 2 to 4

Peruvian Pinto Puree

PERUVIAN SECO

This is one of my most favorite recipes. Seitan cooked in a cilantro broth with potatoes. Seco is traditionally cooked until dry, but I like mine saucy so the rice can absorb all of the delicious broth. It's also really fast to put together for a weeknight meal.

1 ½ cups cubed seitan
1 onion, diced
3 cloves of garlic, minced
2 tablespoons olive oil
2 teaspoons cumin
1 large potato, cubed
4 cups water
2 tablespoons vegetable bouillon base
1 bunch fresh cilantro, lower stems cut and removed
1/2 cup water
Vegan Garlic Aioli (see page 12)
Sunflower sprouts

In a fry pan over medium heat, sauté onion, garlic and seitan in olive oil until lightly browned and the onions turn translucent. Add cumin and sauté for another minute. Add potato, 4 cups of water and the bouillon base. Increase heat to medium high and bring to a low boil, stirring to melt the bouillon base. Reduce heat to medium low and cover so that the Seco just simmers. Immediately cut away lower stems from the cilantro. Put the remaining cilantro (leaves and upper stems) into a blender with 1/2 cup of water. Blend until you have a cilantro sauce. Add half of the cilantro sauce to the simmering pan. Simmer the Seco until potatoes are tender, approximately 15 minutes. Remove from heat. Add the remaining cilantro sauce and stir. Season to taste with salt and pepper. Serve over rice, topped with a dollop of Vegan Garlic Aioli and sunflower sprouts.

Serves 4

Peruvian Seco

PORCINI MUSHROOM RISOTTO WITH PURPLE PERUVIAN POTATOES

I created this dish to blend the flavors of my heritage (Italian) with those of my Peruvian husband.

½ oz. dried Porcini mushrooms
1 ½ cups water
4-5 cups of veggie broth (preferably made from vegetable bouillon base)
2 tablespoons olive oil
1 onion, chopped
1 ½ cups of Arborio rice
2 cloves of garlic, minced
1 teaspoon cumin
1 lb. of baby Portobello mushrooms, chopped
1 16 oz. package of frozen sweet white corn, thawed
1 cup of Roasted Peruvian Purple Potatoes, diced (see page 28)
½ cup Garlic Cashew Cheese (see page 4)
½ cup chopped cilantro

Bring 1 ½ cups of water to a boil. Remove from heat. Add porcini mushrooms and allow to soak until softened. Remove porcini mushrooms from water when soft, chop and set aside. Reserve porcini liquid.

Bring broth to a boil and keep it at a low simmer. Add reserved porcini liquid to the broth.

In a large skillet over medium heat, add 2 tablespoons of olive oil. Add onion and cook until translucent. Add rice, garlic and cumin and sauté for a few more minutes. Add ½ cup of warm broth, ¼ of the mushrooms and ¼ of the corn and stir. Let cook, stirring occasionally until the liquid absorbs. Keep adding approximately ¾ cup of the broth, ¼ of the mushrooms and ¼ of the corn. Cook each addition until the liquid evaporates, stirring occasionally. Cook until the rice is al dente. Add Roasted Peruvian Purple potatoes and heat through. Place ½ cup of the remaining hot broth in a bowl, along with the Garlic Cashew Cheese. Mix together until it melts and add it to the risotto. Add additional broth for a creamier/saucier risotto and immediately remove from heat. Add cilantro. Season to taste with salt and pepper.

Serves 4

Porcini Mushroom Risotto with Purple Peruvian Potatoes

PURE DE PALLARES

This is the ultimate in homey, comfort food. A puree of lima beans, blended with Garlic Cashew Cheese, for extra creamy deliciousness. Serve over rice and steamed kale.

2 ½ cups of dried Lima beans
Water
1 cup of reserved cooking liquid
2 teaspoons vegetable bouillon base
½ cup Garlic Cashew Cheese (see page 4)
1 ½ teaspoons salt

Rinse dried lima beans with water and drain. In a large stockpot (9 quarts), place Lima beans and water to cover by one inch. Bring to a boil and allow to cook for five minutes. Remove from heat. Allow the beans to cool in the water for 1 hour. Drain off excess water from beans. Pour enough fresh water into the stock pot, to cover beans by several inches. Return to boil. Reduce heat to medium, cover, and allow to cook until tender and falling apart. (The smaller Lima beans may cook in as little as 1 hour and 15 minutes. Feel free to cook the beans in a pressure cooker, if you have one). Remove from heat and allow to cool, reserving one cup of the cooking liquid. Add the vegetable bouillon base to the reserved cup of cooking liquid and stir. Drain the rest of the liquid from the pot.

Place the cooked beans, cooking liquid with bouillon base, Garlic Cashew Cheese and salt into a blender and blend. You may have to do this in two batches, depending on the size of your blender. Season to taste with salt and pepper. Serve and devour.

Serves 5 to 6

Pure de Pallares

RAW PERUVIAN SPICED TOMATO SAUCE WITH PASTA

This raw tomato sauce is amazing. The flavors just scream at you! Dry farmed tomatoes from your local farmer's market yield the most flavor, but heirloom tomatoes also work well. You can also serve the sauce over quinoa or potatoes, or as a topping for lettuce wraps.

4 large or 5 medium tomatoes (in season)
Half a bunch of cilantro, stems removed
2-3 tablespoons of sundried tomato paste
2 tablespoons of olive oil
1 teaspoon of balsamic vinegar
1 teaspoon of light agave nectar (optional)
½ teaspoon cumin
¼ teaspoon smoked paprika
Salt and pepper to taste
1 pound of cooked pasta
Vegan Parmesan (see page 14)

Pulse all ingredients in a blender or food processor. Let stand for an hour or so, to thicken the sauce.

Serve over pasta with Vegan Parmesan.

Serves 4

Raw Peruvian Spiced Tomato Sauce with Pasta

ROCOTO RELLENO

Rocoto peppers resemble a red bell pepper, but are fiery and hard to find in the United States. I use a mixture of red, yellow and orange bell peppers, because they are so colorful. The peppers are stuffed with a creamy seitan mixture, and covered in a delectable sauce.

4 red, yellow or orange bell peppers
1 onion, diced
1 clove of garlic, minced
2 tablespoons olive oil
3 cups of seitan, ground with a hand chopper or food processor
1 teaspoon cumin
1 teaspoon salt
½ teaspoon pepper
½ cup walnuts, coarsely chopped
1 tablespoon aji panca paste
1 tablespoon aji amarillo paste
½ cup soy milk
1/3 cup Vegan Parmesan (see page 14)
2 ½ tablespoons Garlic Cashew Cheese (see page 4)
½ cup cilantro, chopped
¾ cup reserved filling
¼ cup Vegan Parmesan (see page 14)
¾ cup soy milk

Preheat oven to 350 degrees.

Cut tops off of bell peppers. Reserve tops. Clean, devein and remove seeds from the inside of the peppers. Set aside.

In a large fry pan over medium heat, sauté onion, garlic and seitan in olive oil, until onion turns translucent. Add cumin, salt, pepper, walnuts, aji panca paste and aji amarillo paste. Cook for another minute. Add soy milk, Vegan Parmesan and Garlic Cashew Cheese. Stir until combined. Add cilantro and remove from heat.

Place bell peppers in a large glass casserole dish that has a lid. Stuff bell peppers with filling. Place tops on bell peppers. Take remaining filling (approximately ¾ of a cup) and place in a blender. Add ¼ cup of Vegan Parmesan and ¾ cup of soy milk. Blend. Pour contents of blender into the casserole dish with the bell peppers. Bake for approximately 45 minutes to 1 hour, or until peppers are tender. Season to taste with salt and pepper.

Serves 4

Rocoto Relleno

TACU TACU

Tacu Tacu is beans and rice formed into a loaf, then fried. A great dish to make with leftover beans and rice. If I was on a deserted island and could only eat two foods for the rest of my life, guess what they would be? Yup, beans and rice!

1 cup of Indian white basmati rice
1 ½ cups of water
1 15 oz. can of refried black beans
½ teaspoon smoked paprika
½ teaspoon garlic powder
1 teaspoon cumin
½ teaspoon of salt
1 tablespoon aji panca paste
Half a bunch of cilantro, chopped
3 tablespoons olive oil
Vegan Garlic Aioli (see page 12)

Bring water to a boil and add rice. Bring to a boil again, reduce heat to low and simmer (covered) for fifteen minutes. Shut off heat and allow rice to rest in the pot for approximately ten to fifteen minutes. Remove cover from pot and allow to cool for another ten minutes.

Gently warm the beans in a small pot. Add the garlic powder, cumin, salt and aji panca paste. Remove from heat.

Put cooked rice into a large bowl. Add half of the beans. Mix the rice and beans until they hold their form and can be shaped. Add more beans if necessary. Add the cilantro. Form into an oblong log, about the size of a slightly flattened fruitcake.

In a large non-stick fry pan, heat 3 tablespoons of olive oil over medium heat. Place the log of rice and beans into the fry pan and cook until browned on all sides. Season to taste with salt and pepper. Serve with Vegan Garlic Aioli or vegan sour cream.

Serves 2

Tacu Tacu

TRIPLE SANDWICH

This popular Peruvian sandwich is pronounced "triPLAY." It's made with avocado, tomato and tasty tofu salad, layered between bread slices. This nutritious sandwich is a great weeknight meal, when you are short on time or when you don't feel like cooking!

2 cups firm tofu, crumbled (use regular tofu and not silken tofu)
1 stalk celery, minced
¾ teaspoon turmeric
½ teaspoon cider vinegar
¾ teaspoon salt
1 teaspoon evaporated cane juice
½ cup Vegan Garlic Aioli (see page 12)
16 slices of vegan sandwich bread, crusts removed
2 avocados, sliced
2 medium tomatoes, sliced
Vegan Garlic Aioli, for spreading (see page 12)

In a medium bowl mix tofu, celery, turmeric, cider vinegar, salt, evaporated cane juice and Vegan Garlic Aioli. Set aside.

Take one piece of bread and top it with ¼ of the tofu mixture. Top with a second slice of bread. Layer 4-5 slices of avocado on top of the second slice of bread. Take a third slice of bread and spread it with Vegan Garlic Aioli. Place the third slice of bread (Vegan Garlic Aioli side facing down) on top of the avocado. Layer 4-5 slices of tomato on top of the third slice of bread. Take a fourth slice of bread and spread it with Vegan Garlic Aioli. Place the fourth slice of bread on top of the tomatoes, with the Vegan Garlic Aioli side facing down. Cut the sandwich into two triangles. Repeat with remaining ingredients.

Makes 4 sandwiches

Triple Sandwich

4. DESSERTS

Peruvians love their desserts........and their cream, butter and eggs........and more eggs. I once saw a recipe with 20 eggs in them, and sadly that can be the norm in Peru! These desserts are super "que rico" with no eggs, dairy or cholesterol. It's a win for the cows, the hens and you! From caramel to chocolate, you'll find your dessert fix in here.

ALFAJORES

YUM!!! WARNING!! These cookies can be highly addictive! Manjar Blanco sandwiched between two cookie wafers. And coated in powdered sugar, too! They are messy, but finger licking good.

1 ½ cups pastry flour (or regular flour)
¼ teaspoon baking powder
3 tablespoons egg replacer (powdered)
2 ½ tablespoons vegan margarine, melted
Manjar Blanco (see page 90)

Preheat oven to 350 degrees. Line a baking sheet with parchment paper.

In a medium bowl, mix flour and baking powder. Place the egg replacer in a 1 cup measuring cup. Add water to almost full (approximately 4/5 of a cup). Mix well. Add egg replacer mixture and margarine to the flour and baking powder. Mix and then knead until incorporated. Place dough between two sheets of parchment paper. Roll out to about 1/8 inch thick. Use a lid (the size that comes with a peanut butter jar) to cut dough into rounds. Place the rounds on the parchment lined baking sheet. Pierce the rounds with a fork. Bake for approximately 12 to 15 minutes. Allow to cool thoroughly.

To assemble, place a couple of tablespoons of Manjar Blanco (or more) on a round. Top with another round, so you have a sandwich. Roll cookie in powdered sugar. Repeat with the remaining rounds and the Manjar Blanco.

Makes approximately 8 Alfajores.

Alfajores

ARROZ CON SOY AND COCONUT LECHE

The ultimate in comfort dessert..........rice pudding! This version is even better for you, since it contains NO dairy. Rice pudding made with soy milk, soy creamer and coconut milk..........topped off with vanilla and cinnamon. YUM.

¾ cup Indian basmati white rice
1 ½ cups water
Pinch of salt
¾ teaspoon cinnamon
2 ½ cups soy milk
½ cup soy creamer
1 cup coconut milk
2/3 cup evaporated cane juice
½ cup raisins
1 teaspoon vanilla extract

In a medium saucepan, bring water, rice, salt and cinnamon to a boil. Reduce heat to low and cover. Cook for ten minutes. Add soy milk, soy creamer, coconut milk, evaporated cane juice and raisins. Bring to low boil. Cover, reduce heat and allow to simmer for 30 minutes. Remove from heat and add vanilla. Serve warm, cold or at room temperature.

Serves 4

DECADENT CHOCOLATE RICE PUDDING

This dish is a must for chocolate lovers. It takes Arroz con Soy and Coconut Leche to new heights! It's like having a warm bowl of hot cocoa!

Arroz con Soy and Coconut Leche (see page 86)
½ cup to ¾ cup of vegan chocolate chips

Prepare Arroz con Soy and Coconut Leche per directions. During the last couple minutes of cooking, add the vegan chocolate chips (more or less, depending on how much chocolate you like). Allow chocolate to melt and stir. Serve warm.

Arroz con Soy and Coconut Leche

MANJAR BLANCO

This caramel like pudding is eaten as a dessert with a spoon, or as a filling for cakes or cookies. It's really sweet, so you don't need to eat a lot to get your dessert fix. My husband and his sister used to have contests when they were kids, to see who could make the pudding last longest on their spoons.

2 ½ cups of soy milk
2 ½ cups of evaporated cane juice
1 teaspoon vanilla extract

In a large saucepan over medium heat, stir the soy milk and evaporated cane juice together. Bring to a simmer over medium heat, stirring occasionally. When it comes to a constant simmer, this is when you need to really start working! Turn down the heat just until it's a little below the medium setting. With a wooden spoon, stir constantly. You will see the sugar melt and the soy milk get thicker. Eventually you will see the top half of the mixture turn a lighter color, as it simmers. Continue to stir the mixture. The caramel is done when you can cut a path through the mixture with your spoon (and it stays that way briefly) before it recedes. This may take anywhere from 30 to 45 minutes, depending on the stove and heat level. Remove from heat and add vanilla extract. Immediately pour into a heat resistant glass container and allow to cool thoroughly.

Makes approximately 2 cups.

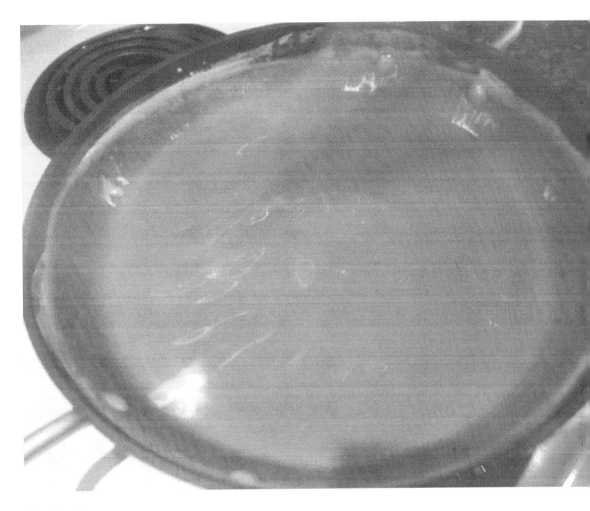

Manjar Blanco

PERUVIAN DARK CHOCOLATE CANDY BAR COOKIES WITH SEA SALT

Crunchy on the outside and gooey in the middle, with just the right amount of sweet and salt. YUM!

½ cup vegan margarine, softened
½ cup brown sugar
3/8 cup evaporated cane juice
1 ½ tablespoons water
1 teaspoon vanilla extract
1 cup flour
¾ cup rolled oats, pulverized into a powder in the blender
½ teaspoon baking soda
½ teaspoon salt
One 3oz. bar of Peruvian (vegan) dark chocolate bar, cut into shreds and tiny chunks
Sea salt

Preheat oven to 350. Line a baking sheet with parchment paper.

Combine margarine, brown sugar, evaporated cane juice, water and vanilla and mix well. Add dry ingredients and mix thoroughly. Add chopped candy bar. Bake on parchment lined cookie sheet for ten minutes. Remove from oven. Press down lightly with a spatula. Sprinkle lightly with sea salt.

Makes approximately 16 cookies.

Peruvian Dark Chocolate Candy Bar Cookies with Sea Salt

PIONONO

A delicious sponge cake filled with caramel pudding, and rolled up jelly roll style. Topped with powdered sugar. It makes a beautiful dessert for a special occasion, or just for you to eat alone in the corner when no one else is home.

2 cups of flour
1/3 cup of evaporated cane juice
2 teaspoons of baking powder
¼ cup agave nectar
¼ cup maple syrup
1 cup of soy milk or nut milk
Egg replacer powder (to equal two eggs)
¼ cup of olive oil
Powdered sugar
Manjar Blanco (see page 90)

Preheat oven to 350 degrees. Line a 13" x 9" baking pan with parchment paper.

In a large mixing bowl, stir flour, evaporated cane juice and baking powder together. Add agave nectar, maple syrup, soy milk, egg replacer and oil. Stir to combine. Spread into parchment lined pan. Bake for 10-15 minutes. Remove from oven and allow to cool for ten minutes. Sprinkle the top with some powdered sugar and roll up jelly roll style (with the parchment paper intact). Allow to cool completely. When cooled, unroll. Spread with Manjar Blanco. Roll back up jelly roll style (without the parchment paper). Dust entire roll with powdered sugar. Cut into slices and serve.

Serves 8

Pionono

SWEET PASTEL DE CHOCLO

This sweet corn dessert is somewhere between a flan and a cheesecake, in both texture and flavor. After it comes out of the oven, it won't be completely set. Don't worry, as it cools it sets. It's best to let it firm up completely in the refrigerator overnight. If you need it right away, you can put it in the freezer for a couple of hours, to speed up the process.

1 cup soy milk
2 cups corn kernels
¼ cup agave nectar
¼ cup maple syrup
Powdered egg replacer for 5 eggs
1/3 cup vegan margarine
¾ cup vegan cream cheese

Preheat oven to 350 degrees. Grease and flour a 9" spring form pan.

Blend all ingredients in a blender. Pour into pan and bake for 65 minutes. Remove from oven and let cool completely. Refrigerate overnight before serving. Serve cold, right out of the refrigerator.

Serves 8

Sweet Pastel de Choclo

SOY & COCONUT LECHE CAKE (TRES LECHES CAKE)

This cake is awesome! It's a cross between a cake and a super creamy pudding! Make sure you use parchment paper, otherwise you won't be able to cut your cake. This cake needs to be refrigerated at all times, and served right out of the refrigerator. The most fun way to eat it is with 8 friends and 8 spoons.............all out of the pan!

2 cups evaporated cane juice
¼ cup vegan margarine, melted
¼ cup soy milk
1 teaspoon vanilla
Egg replacer, equal to 5 eggs
2 cups flour
1 tablespoon baking powder
1 ¼ cup soy creamer
2 cups soy milk
1 cup coconut milk
¼ cup maple syrup

Preheat oven to 350 degrees. Line a 9" x 13" baking pan with parchment paper.

In a large bowl, mix evaporated cane juice, vegan margarine, ¼ cup soy milk, vanilla and egg replacer mixture. Add flour and baking powder. Pour into prepared pan. Bake for 25 minutes.

While cake is baking, mix soy creamer, 2 cups soy milk, coconut milk and maple syrup in a large bowl. Set aside.

When cake is done, remove from oven and allow to cool for 5 minutes. Poke holes in cake with a toothpick. Pour soy creamer, soy milk, coconut milk and maple syrup mixture over the top of the cake, while it's still hot. Make sure to distribute it evenly. Allow to cool for approximately 30 minutes. Refrigerate for at least 4 hours, prior to serving. Serve cold, right out of the refrigerator.

Serves 8

Soy & Coconut Leche Cake

5. SPECIAL INGREDIENTS LIST

Definitions of some of the ingredients that you might not be familiar with, and where to find them.

Special Ingredients List

The following are a few ingredients that might be new to your kitchen, and are included in various recipes in this book:

Agave nectar: A sweet syrup made from the agave plant. Can be substituted for maple syrup or honey in recipes. Agave nectar can be found in the sweetener aisle at your natural food store.

Aji amarillo and aji panca pastes: Pastes that are made from various hot peppers of Peru. The pastes come in a jar and can be found at some natural food stores, in the ethnic food section. You can also buy them online, and sometimes at Latin American markets.

Braggs Liquid Aminos: Braggs is a liquid protein concentrate, comes in a plastic bottle, and tastes much better than soy sauce! Braggs can be found by the soy sauces, at your natural food store.

Egg replacer: Egg replacer comes in liquid or powdered forms. I like the powdered form made from potato starch and tapioca. Egg replacer can be found in the baking aisle at your natural food store.

Evaporated cane juice: A more natural form of sugar that is less processed than bleached, white sugar. Evaporated cane juice is sold in packages in the sweetener aisle, or in the bulk section of your natural food store. Raw cane sugar or organic sugar can also be substituted for evaporated cane juice.

Garbanzo bean flour: Also known as chickpea flour, it's the flour made from garbanzo beans. Garbanzo bean flour can be found in the bulk section of your natural food store.

Miso: Fermented soybean paste. Miso imparts a savory and salty flavor to dishes. Miso can be found in the refrigerated section at your natural food store, usually next to the refrigerated condiments.

Nutritional yeast: Imparts a cheesy flavor to foods. It is a non-active type of yeast and is loaded with Vitamin B-12. It comes in large or small flake form and is located in the bulk section at your natural food store.

Purple Peruvian potatoes: These potatoes are easy to see, since they are purple! They can be found in many grocery stores and in most natural food stores.

Seitan: Otherwise known as "wheat meat" since it's made from vital wheat gluten (the protein of the flour). Seitan has a great texture, flavor and appearance. If purchased, it comes in cubes, slices or strips, but it's super easy to make from scratch. Seitan is located in the refrigerated section (with the other meat analogues) at your natural food store.

Vegan chorizo: Typically made from soy, with a taste that's very authentic. It can be found in the refrigerated section of your natural food store, by the other meat analogues.

Vegan Garlic Aioli: Although I have included a recipe for this in the cookbook, there are some vegan aioli's that you can find in the refrigerated section at your natural food store. There are also vegan mayo's out there, which are found in the refrigerated section at your natural food store. Shop around, as there are a few that are superior to other brands...........and some brands taste..........well...........ahem, not very good. However, I would urge you to make the homemade version in this cookbook, as it is super delicious!

Vegetable bouillon base: A bouillon base that comes in a jar in a paste form, and is used like a bouillon cube. The base is melted into boiling water and added to a recipe. You can find the base at natural food stores and at many regular grocery stores, in the soup and broth aisle. You can also substitute vegetable broth for the paste in any of the recipes, although the bouillon base has a superior flavor.

6. INDEX

INDEX

ABOUT THE AUTHOR

Vicki Cosio lives in Northern California with her husband and rescued pups. Her passion is promoting veganism by being an example in her sport, and in her cooking.

Made in the USA
Lexington, KY
06 November 2015